Upside Living in a Downside Economy

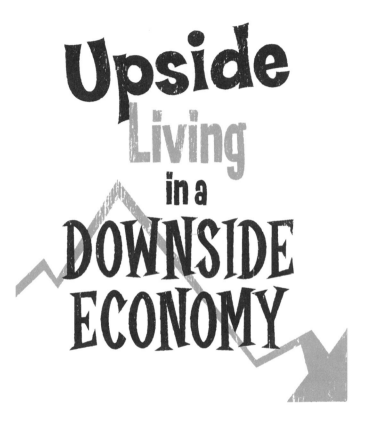

Upside Living in a DOWNSIDE ECONOMY

MIKE SLAUGHTER

ABINGDON PRESS
Nashville, Tennessee

Library of Congress Cataloging-in-Publication Data

Slaughter, Michael.
 Living upside in a downside economy / Michael B. Slaughter.
   p. cm.
 ISBN 978-1-4267-0305-8 (pbk. : alk. paper)
 1. Economics--Religious aspects--Christianity. 2. Finance, Personal--Religious aspects--Christianity.
I. Title.
 BR115.E3S57 2009
 241'.68--dc22

2009008705

CONTENTS

Introduction

We have an incredible God who cares about the little details in our lives. One of the mistakes people often make is that they think God cares mostly about "later," as in eternity. But God also cares about the success of God's children in this life. The Greek word *sozo*, which we translate "salvation," means "wellness." God desires wellness in every area of our lives.

Not long ago I received my 401(k) statement in the mail. As a pastor, I am self-employed. So I have no pension apart from Social Security and what I can do in my 401(k), in which I have been investing since 1972. I was a little afraid to open the statement. All I can say is that what I saw was ugly. I realized that the statement was only through the end of September and did not even include what have been, to date, the worst months in the history of the stock market.

Perhaps you have had a similar experience in recent months. Our response to the current financial crisis tends to be reactive, coming out of the twin emotions of fear and worry. Yet we must remember that those emotions are not logical. No matter what industry does, there is only one thing that can create a downturn in the stock market, and that is fear and worry. Unfortunately, it seems there is plenty of that to go around these days.

The current financial crisis is impacting every age group. Twenty-five- to thirty-four-year-olds hold the second highest rate of bankruptcy. Baby-boomers, who are now fifty-six to sixty-five years old—years that should be a critical saving time—are continuing to live like Americans with a negative savings rate. Those of us who are in this age range continue to spend more than we earn. The average baby-boomer has over $40,000 in consumer debt, and that does not include a home mortgage.

Not only is this current crisis combining with poor money habits to create the toxic emotions of fear and worry, but it also is a source of incredible conflict in relationships. Studies show that more than half of all divorces are the result of financial tension.

My aim in this book is to help all of us live beyond these challenging circumstances and experience the abundant life for which God created us. I want to challenge followers of Christ to be a redemptive influence in the world through our own biblical priorities and practices, so that we could be a community offering hope in the lives of others during this turbulent economic time. In each chapter we will look at a passage from the Book of James, a book of practical, applicable faith for hard times. The New Testament churches to whom James wrote were dealing with harsh economic conditions as well as severe persecution. James' teaching is applicable today in learning how to live above our situations as well.

> **Don't just *believe* what God says in the Bible; *trust* what God says, and then put it into practice!**

I challenge you to make a commitment to action. Don't just *believe* what God says in the Bible; *trust* what God says, and then put it into practice! I am passionately convinced that you can live upside in a downside economy when you put your faith into action by practicing the timeless biblical principles addressed in this book.

SEEKING GOD'S PERSPECTIVE

SEEKING GOD'S PERSPECTIVE

*Those conflicts and disputes among you, where do they
come from? Do they not come from your cravings that are
at war within you? You want something and do not have it;
so you commit murder. And you covet something and cannot
obtain it; so you engage in disputes and conflicts. You do
not have, because you do not ask. You ask and do not receive, because you ask wrongly, in order to spend what you
get on your pleasures. Adulterers! Do you not know that
friendship with the world is enmity with God? Therefore
whoever wishes to be a friend of the world becomes an
enemy of God. Or do you suppose that it is for nothing that
the scripture says, "God yearns jealously for the spirit that
he has made to dwell in us"? But he gives all the more
grace; therefore it says, "God opposes the proud, but gives
grace to the humble." (James 4:1-6)*

If we truly desire to build sound financial health, we must
begin by building a foundation that is firmly grounded in God's
perspective on wealth and finances. We must earnestly search
for what God has to say about wealth and money. Checking
God's perspective comes by looking to God's Word. Yet before

Financial freedom begins with knowing who God is.

we can respond appropriately to God's perspective on financial matters, we must be sure that we have a right understanding of who God is. We must know God's character in order to trust God; only that trust enables us to put God's principles into practice. Financial freedom begins with knowing who God is, because financial freedom is based in trusting God's character and intentions toward us.

Check God's Character

Many of us struggle when it comes to the subject of God and finances because we do not understand who God truly is. We have a picture of God as a moralistic judge-creator. Yet Jesus taught us to pray, "Our *Father . . .*" (Matthew 6:9). This opening address of the Lord's Prayer is a reminder that God is a powerful parent who actively seeks the well-being of God's children. As a matter of fact, again and again Jesus reminded us of the fatherly kindness of God. In Matthew 7 we read, "Everyone who asks [God] receives, and everyone who searches finds, and for everyone who knocks, the door will be opened. . . . If you then, who are evil, know how to give good gifts to your children, how much more will your Father in heaven give good things to those who ask him!" (verses 8, 11).

When my son, Jonathan, went to college, I had a black 1960 Corvette with silver coves and a white convertible top. It had been completely redone, and I loved having and driving this car. But then I sold it. Why? Because my son's well-being—specifically, his education—was more important than that Corvette. Now he is a third-year medical school student!

One day Carolyn and I were watching the news. They were reporting that many college loans will be cancelled because the banks that are receiving government bail-out money are using it for bonuses and buyouts of other banks. As a result, a lot of students will not be able to get loans. Carolyn looked at me and said, "What happens if Jonathan's loan for medical school is cancelled?" I said, "Carolyn, our house is mostly paid for, so even if we took a major hit on selling our house, we would get enough money out of it to pay for the rest of his medical school. We can live in an apartment."

The heart of a loving parent does whatever is required for the sake of the child.

Jesus was saying that if we have this kind of love for our children, how much more will our Father in heaven—whose love for us is infinitely greater and purer—give good things to those who ask. The New Testament is filled with similar promises. In Philippians we read: "My God will meet all your needs according to his glorious riches in Christ Jesus" (4:19, NIV). Isn't that an amazing Father! Likewise, in Romans 8:32 we find this promise: "He who did not spare his own Son, but gave him up for us all—how will he not also, along with him, graciously give us all things?" (NIV).

This reality of God as our loving Father is powerful, which is why I pray the Lord's Prayer aloud in my study each day.

The next words in the prayer are equally powerful: "Our Father *in heaven*" (Matthew 6:9). "Our Father" reminds us who God is. "In heaven" reminds us what God has. To put it another way, God owns the universe. God created the cosmos. All things in heaven and on earth are owned by God. In other words, not only do we have the love of our eternal parent, God has the resources to back all of God's promises. Financial freedom begins right here, and it is based in trust. When we trust God's promises, we are able to practice God's directives.

I do not believe in prosperity theology—the idea that you follow Jesus to get rich. That is self-centered and self-focused. But I do believe that God desires our success. Every good parent desires the success and well-being of his or her children. If my kids could make $40,000 a year or $100,000 a year, what would I choose? I would choose $100,000 if they could earn it by serving God's purpose and serving humanity. I desire the best for my children. Our infinite God cares even more about our well-being and is deeply invested in bringing about God's best will for our lives. Nothing is beyond God's provision for us.

Check God's Perspective

The Bible not only tells us who God is; it also gives us the promises and principles of God. It teaches us God's perspective on everything from morality, salvation, and eternal life to practical matters such as finances. In fact, there are hundreds of financial directives in the Bible. For example, we are told that debt is not our friend. The Bible says the debtor is always slave to the lender (Proverbs 22:7). Here is the problem with debt: When you have debt of any kind in your life, you are working today to pay for the past, instead of creating the future. That is why debt is not our friend. The Bible also says that we should never co-sign a loan for another person (Proverbs 11:15; 17:18; 22:26-27). But the basis of all financial wisdom and health begins with this essential principle: *We are to practice planned giving to God.* We will discuss this principle at length in the next chapter. For now,

> **When you have debt of any kind in your life, you are working today to pay for the past, instead of creating the future.**

we will generalize by saying that we must put God first when it comes to our finances.

When we put God first and serve God with our money, money serves us. That is exactly what this verse means: "Seek first the kingdom of God and His righteousness, and all these things shall be added to you" (Matthew 6:33, NKJV). "All these things" refers to the physical provision of God on our behalf. We don't have to worry about multiplying wealth because God has promised that to us. But if we serve money instead of God, we will always be slaves to the past, because we will be working for our possessions instead of working for our Creator. God has promised to supply all we need if we will put God first in our lives.

I am not worried or afraid in the midst of this financial crisis because I know that my only job is to serve God's purpose. God has promised to provide all my needs if I follow God and seek to live according to God's principles. So, I continue to invest in my 401(k) every two weeks because I know that God will provide all my needs. This kind of perspective is possible only because of the power of the Word of God. We must continually come back to the Word and check God's perspective.

Check Your Motives

In addition to checking God's perspective, we must check our own motives. James 4:3 says, "You ask and do not receive." Sometimes we simply fail to ask. Other times we do ask God, but nothing happens. Perhaps the reason we do not receive is because we ask with wrong motives so that we may spend what we get on our own pleasures. Our motives are the compelling force or energy behind all our actions. Our motives drive our actions.

Our motives are the compelling force or energy behind all our actions.

Note the word at the end of James 4:3: *pleasures*. The word in Greek is *hedonism*. Hedonism is an ancient Greek philosophy that was articulated in the fifth and fourth centuries B.C. by a disciple of Socrates named Aristippus. Aristippus taught that the pursuit of pleasure is the ultimate objective in life. He said that pursuing pleasure is why we work hard. Today, we work overtime so that we can buy boats and go to the lake and have a lot of toys. Aristippus said that minimizing pain and maximizing pleasure is what life is all about. This philosophy is in stark contrast to the worldview of Jesus Christ, which the apostle Paul expressed this way: "I want to know Christ and the power of his resurrection and the sharing of his sufferings" (Philippians 3:10).

We are never going to know the power of the resurrection in any dimension in our lives—in our marriages, our relationships, our work, or our finances—until we are willing to go through the pain, to experience the discipline. We can sum it up this way: No pain, no gain. This hedonistic philosophy has created a Christian hedonism that has infiltrated the church. People have come up to me after worship and said, "Mike, I don't know what is going on with me. I used to really enjoy worship. It was such an incredible experience. It was like tingles went through my body. Now I am not experiencing anything." They were seeking a pleasurable experience instead of seeking God.

So often we profess Jesus Christ but continue to pursue the values of our materialistic culture. It is like the rich young entrepreneur who came to Jesus and asked, "What must I do to inherit eternal life?" (Mark 10:17). Jesus responded by mentioning some commandments. The young man said that he had kept the commandments.

Like many Christian hedonists today, the rich young man was committed to moral living. Yet even though he was pursuing Jesus and was committed to moral living, he still found his values in hedonism, in the pursuit of pleasure. We know this because of what comes next in the story.

In Mark 10, Jesus said to the young man, "If you wish to be complete, sell your possessions." I don't believe Jesus meant for him to literally sell everything he had. Rather, I believe Jesus meant that he needed to let go of what he was holding onto in his attempt to find meaning and security. Jesus essentially said, "Let go of where you are trying to find life, and focus on the things that God cares about. Then come and follow me."

The motive of hedonism creates a spirit of coveting. Coveting means to want what we don't have, which often leads to debt. Coveting is failing to celebrate the blessings of what we have been given, and it always leads to conflict. In any dimension of our lives, when we fail to see and celebrate the blessings that God has already given us, we inevitably begin to seek satisfaction in other sources. James calls us adulterous people (4:4) because coveting is adultery (disloyalty) against God.

Jesus said, "*I* am the bread of life. Whoever comes to me will never be hungry, and whoever believes in me will never be thirsty" (John 6:34-35). When we fail to see the blessings of what we have in Jesus Christ and seek satisfaction somewhere else, we are saying that Jesus is not enough. But the truth is that we can lose everything we have and still have enough if we have Jesus Christ.

The idea is not that *having* money and possessions is bad. It is *loving* money, or seeking security in money, that we must guard against. The Bible warns, "The *love* of money is a root of all kinds of evil" (1 Timothy 6:10). Likewise, the Book of Hebrews instructs, "Keep your lives free from the *love* of money, and be content with what you have; for [Jesus] has said, 'I will never leave you or forsake you' " (13:5). With that promise, we truly can be content! We are in a good place!

So, we must continually ask God, "Do I have the right motive?" We also must continually ask God to help us stay motivated.

Check the Source of Your Motivation

Many people start something with the right motive but never finish what they started because they don't stay motivated. Motivation is the ongoing force or energy that propels each action toward the next accomplishment. We simply must stay motivated. But where does motivation come from?

James gives us the answer in these words: "But [God] gives . . . more grace" (4:6). Motivation comes from grace, and grace comes from God. Grace is something we do not deserve or earn; it is a gift. This is why James ends the verse with these words, "God opposes the proud, but gives grace to the humble."

Have you ever tried to get out of debt only to get frustrated and give up? Have you ever started a diet with the right motive only to quit? What happened? It is called fatigue. How do we stay motivated? God gives us "more grace." God knows that we will fail multiple times, and God's provision is grace.

Some of us have experienced failure in the area of finances. Others of us have experienced failure in other areas. Eight years ago I made a commitment to exercise and eat healthy, and I am sticking with it. Yet sometimes I fail to exercise or eat right. Despite my failures, however, God's grace enables me to keep on keeping on.

My family recently celebrated my birthday and my future daughter-in-law's birthday at the same time at my sister's house. My wife, Carolyn, made an apple pie for my future daughter-in-law, Stacy, and a cherry pie for me. My sister, Gayle, also made her incredible homemade ice cream. That is one addiction I have. I can pass on regular ice cream, but there is something about homemade ice cream! So on my birthday I had apple pie, cherry pie, and two big bowls of homemade ice cream! However, it is not my practice to do this. That occasion might be called a failure, but it was not the beginning of a habit. I am thankful that God gives us more grace.

When it comes to pursuing financial health, a lot of us start with the right motive but fail to stay motivated. Where does lasting motivation come from? It comes from the Lord. Our dependence must be on God alone. We can't manufacture motivation. Even when we fail, God's grace is what sustains us and enables us to persevere.

Whether it's our health or our finances or any other area of our lives, God gives us more grace.

Check Who You Are Listening To

Finally, we must check who we are listening to on a regular basis. A good friend of mine, Ross, is in automobile sales. Of all the professions that are experiencing greater challenges during these trying economic times, automobile sales is surely one of them. But there are some people who always find a way with God. Recently, I said to Ross, "I have known you for many years, and I have never seen you not find a way with God to sell cars. How many cars have you sold this month?"

It was three days before the end of the month at the time. Ross said, "I have sold twelve this month." Now, that would be considered good in a stable economy, so it's beyond good in the current economy! Then he added, "My goal is fifteen." I asked him to tell me how he does it. His answer was simple: "I don't listen to the media."

> **To keep our motivation, we must be careful to whom we are listening.**

To keep our motivation, we must be careful to whom we are listening. This is why I am continually aware of what I am putting into my mind. The first thing I put in my mind every day is the Word of God. Regardless of what all the indicators say across the globe, I daily feed my mind and my spirit with the Word of God. The other folks I am listening to, including the people whose books I am reading, are those who are demonstrating godly fruitfulness in their lives.

Take advantage of every opportunity you have to gain financial insights and wisdom. Anyone who desires to build sound financial health seeks wise counsel. My wife, Carolyn, and I have been blessed to have people in our lives who have taught us wise financial counsel, beginning with professors I had in college and seminary who sat down and taught me basic principles about debt and interest rates. Who are the people in *your* life who can provide wise financial counsel? What opportunities are available to you for financial instruction? Talk with people you know and respect who are knowledgeable in the area of finances. Look for books you might read, workshops or seminars you might attend, courses you might take, or Bible study groups you might join. Consider the benefits of consulting with a financial advisor. Follow the advice of Proverbs 1:5, which says, "Let the wise listen and add to their learning, / and let the discerning get guidance" (NIV), and you will be on your way to achieving financial health!

Remember, if you are living in defeat in the area of your finances, you don't have to stay there! Regardless of how far you may be in debt or how bleak your situation may be, God can make the impossible possible. It always begins with having the right perspective—God's perspective—and then building on that perspective by keeping the right motives, staying motivated, and seeking wise counsel.

Rebalancing Life Investments

Rebalancing Life Investments

Submit yourselves therefore to God. Resist the devil, and he will flee from you. Draw near to God, and he will draw near to you. Cleanse your hands, you sinners, and purify your hearts, you double-minded. Lament and mourn and weep. Let your laughter be turned into mourning and your joy into dejection. Humble yourselves before the Lord, and he will exalt you. (James 4:7-10)

There is an economic cloud hovering over us these days, yet there is a silver lining to this cloud: Economic challenges cause us to re-examine our financial priorities and practices. You might say that they cause us to evaluate our priorities and rebalance our life investments. If we're willing, hard times help us figure out what is really important in all of life and how to invest more wisely in our relationships, vocation, and God-purpose, as well as our finances.

> **Draw near to God, and he will draw near to you.**
>
> (James 4:8)

It is amazing how many verses in the Bible deal with money. In fact, twenty-seven out of forty-three parables deal with money or possessions. Consider just some of the counsel the Bible gives us regarding money and possessions:

Be sure you know the condition of your flocks,
give careful attention to your herds. (Proverbs 27:23, NIV)

Anyone who tills the land will have plenty of bread,
but one who follows worthless pursuits will have plenty
of poverty. (Proverbs 28:19)

Dishonest money dwindles away,
but he who gathers money little by little makes it grow.
(Proverbs 13:11, NIV)

Be not one of those who give pledges,
who put up security for debts.
If you have nothing with which to pay,
why should your bed be taken from under you?
(Proverbs 22:26-27, ESV)

The wicked borrow, and do not pay back,
but the righteous are generous and keep giving.
(Psalm 37:21)

What I love about verses such as these is that they communicate simple truths for simple folks. In these verses, as well as throughout the Scriptures, we see this principle at work: When we have right priorities and commit to right actions, we're going to realize right results.

Right Priorities + Right Actions = Right Results

This is certainly true in the area of money management. In fact, this is the formula for rebalancing our life investments. Let's explore what this formula involves.

Right Priorities

In the fourth chapter of James, we find some helpful insights that we can relate to the concept of right priorities. First, setting right priorities begins with submitting to God. James states boldly, "Submit yourselves . . . to God" (verse 7). Note that *submit* does not mean "take under advisement." Actually, it is a much stronger word meaning "defer, surrender, or yield." When we submit ourselves to God, we defer our agenda to God's agenda; we surrender our practices to God's practices; we yield our priorities to God's priorities.

Next, James says we are to "resist the devil, and he will flee from [us]" (verse 7). Submitting to God and resisting evil seem to go hand in hand. You see, anywhere God is working—anywhere we are submitting to God's will and God's ways—evil is sure to attack. James makes it clear, however, that resisting—which is standing firm in what we know to be right and true—is the way to defeat temptation every time. He says that if we will draw near to God, God will draw near to us.

The problem is that we human beings are sinful and double-minded, which James acknowledges. He likes to use the word *double-minded*. Earlier in his book, James says that the double-minded should not expect to receive anything from the Lord (1:7-8). Here, in James 4, he is telling those of us who are

29

double-minded to purify our hearts; to grieve, mourn, and wail; and to change our laughter into mourning and our joy to gloom (verse 9). In other words, we are to repent. What James is describing is actually a posture of repentant prayer common to the Jewish people of his day. Such prayers were somber and physical, involving the whole body. Submitting to God clearly involves repentance. James says that those who humble themselves in this way before the Lord will be lifted up.

So, James outlines three steps for us—submitting to God, resisting evil or temptation, and repenting—steps that are integral to the process of rebalancing our priorities.

My financial investment advisor frequently talks to me about another kind of rebalancing—*financial rebalancing*. In light of the current economic environment, I certainly have been doing some financial rebalancing lately! I hope you have, too. Our nation is in the midst of a period of economic correction and, I believe, a period of spiritual correction as well. Now is the time to examine and rebalance our life investments—our priorities—as well as our budgets and bank accounts. This kind of spiritual exercise requires us to humble ourselves before God and take God's Word seriously.

The worst kind of fool is the person who believes that God exists but who lives as if God's directives are not to be taken seriously. We all know people who believe in God but who don't practice God's directives. As we've seen, James calls them double-minded. They try to live with their feet on two different planes—with two conflicting worldviews. These two opposing worldviews are hedonism and Christianity.

We were introduced to the worldview of hedonism in the previous chapter. As we saw, Aristippus, a disciple of Socrates, articulated this philosophy in the fifth and fourth centuries B.C. Simply put, it sets the pursuit of pleasure as the primary goal in life. According to this philosophy, pleasure is the reason we work. The goal is to minimize pain and maximize pleasure. Although hedonism is an ancient philosophy, it is actually a dominant worldview in our culture today, often called materialism. It is a worldview that places self and self's wants at the center. I determine my own priorities, my own values, my own wants, and my own directions; I do what I want, I go where I want, and I buy what I want. If there's anything left over, I may give some to God and others. But I make the decision. In contemporary terms, hedonism is a materialistic worldview that says meaning and security come from things, which creates in us a consumer identity.

Consider Christmas in our culture today, for example. Christmas has become a hedonistic feast of materialistic gluttony. I often say that Christmas is not our birthday; it is Jesus' birthday. We should stop acting as if it's our birthday. We should honor ourselves and our children on our respective birthdays, but we should do what honors Jesus on Jesus' birthday. Yet most Christians tend to miss the real meaning of Christmas and continue its celebration through self-focused practices that fulfill the materialistic desires of their friends and family.

We are double-minded. We try to hang onto the materialistic worldview of the culture while professing the worldview of the kingdom of God. Anytime we say yes to Jesus—and remember, saying yes to Jesus is more than saying we believe he exists, because even the demons in hell believe that he exists—we are making a commitment to follow in *all* his ways.

Anytime we say yes to Jesus, we are making a commitment to follow in *all* his ways.

His values become our values, his priorities become our priorities, and his worldview becomes our worldview. We can be sure that when we make this commitment, to submit ourselves to Jesus Christ, evil is going to come against us. So we must be ready to resist the force that would attempt to paralyze us from fulfilling the purpose of God in our lives.

The story of Jesus in the wilderness can help us to be ready. When Jesus was seeking the will of God in the wilderness for forty days, he was fasting. Therefore, his primary purpose was to fully submit himself to the will of the Father. During that time, Jesus experienced three temptations, and we can relate each temptation to a financial temptation we face today.

First, Jesus was hungry, and the devil's temptation was to turn stones into bread. For us, the temptation is to spend in response to our appetite—to do with our money what we feel will satisfy our hunger at the moment. Have you ever come home with a new car when you weren't looking for one? Have you ever bought a new TV or computer when you really didn't need one? The first temptation is always to spend out of your appetite, not out of your need.

Next, the devil took Jesus to the highest point in Jerusalem and told him to jump off. In Matthew 4, he told Jesus, "Surely because you are his Son, God will send his angels to deliver you." Jesus replied, "You shouldn't tempt the Lord your God." Here's the application for us. We continue to do stupid things with our money and expect God to deliver us from our stupidity. Jesus was no dummy. He knew that you don't tempt the Lord. So, when God gives us a directive about debt, we simply cannot ignore it and expect God to deliver us from our own stupidity.

Finally, Satan had Jesus stand on a high mountain and look at all the kingdoms of the world and all they contain. He said, "If you will follow me, I will give you all this stuff. And you won't even have to sacrifice or go through pain to get it." Jesus replied that we are to worship the Lord and serve him only. The application for us is that we are to bring every dimension of our lives into submission to the kingdom of God worldview expressed in the teachings of Jesus Christ. In other words, we are to make a commitment to stand firm in God's will and resist temptation; and when we do, evil will flee from us. We are to draw near to God, and God will draw near to us.

The bottom line is that anything less than the will of God in every dimension of our financial lives is not an option. We must say, "Lord, I want what you want, and by the strength that comes through your grace, I'm willing to work at it until I do it." That's what it means to stand firm. Defeat is not an option. We must choose to submit to the directives of God.

That is rebalancing our priorities, and the result is right priorities!

Right Actions

Once we have right priorities based on God's directives, we must add right actions. James says that faith without action is useless (2:26). Faith that is not applied in works is powerless. So, let's consider seven right actions related to managing our money that have their roots in the Bible. Note that I didn't say seven *principles*. We know all kinds of principles, but principles do us no good if we don't commit them to action. The following seven actions will lead to right results in our lives and our finances. Remember, right priorities plus right actions equals right results!

1. Do the first "right" thing: planned giving to God.

Before you do anything else in your life, the first "right" thing is planned giving toward God's kingdom work. In the apostle Paul's first letter to the Corinthians we read, "Now about the collection for God's people. . . . On the first day of every week, . . . set aside a sum of money in keeping with [your] income, saving it up" (16:1-2, NIV). What does this mean for us? It means that when we plan our money practices, the first action we should take is planned giving to God. This action recognizes God's rightful ownership of all we have. The Bible says the earth and everything it contains belong to the Lord (Psalm 89:11). What we hold in our hands is not ours. It belongs to the Lord and is the trust of God to us, and we are accountable to the Lord for everything we have. When our first action in the area of finances is giving to God, we demonstrate our trust in God's promise to provide. Jesus said, "I am the bread of life. Whoever comes to me will never be hungry, and whoever believes in me will never be thirsty" (John 6:35).

I don't know about you, but I don't keep my money under a mattress. I take it to the bank. Why? I trust that the bank will deliver on its promise to take care of my money and increase its value by adding interest. And if I trust a bank that is struggling right now more than I trust my mattress, that's saying something!

Yet God is the most secure guarantee of all for my provision. Jesus said it plainly: "Seek first the kingdom of God and His righteousness"—that means seeking first everything that's right according to God's design—"and all these things shall be added to you" (Matthew 6:33, NKJV).

Actually, it is impossible to seek after things and God at the same time. Jesus said we cannot serve both God and money (Matthew 6:24). The apostle Paul expressed it well when he said that "the love of money is a root of all kinds of evil" (1 Timothy 6:10). *Money* itself is not evil; *serving* money is what is evil. Yet when we trust God's love and provision, there is no need to be focused on seeking things. We recognize God's ownership and willingly release our resources to Jesus' lordship.

In the third chapter of Malachi, we read about the importance of giving to God the biblical tithe, which is the first 10 percent of our income. God essentially says to the people, "You are robbing me." The people ask, "How are we robbing you?" And God answers, "In your tithes and offerings." Then in the tenth verse, God tells them to "bring the whole tithe into the storehouse, that there may be food in my house" (NIV).

Some people today think a tithe is anything you put in the offering plate. Actually, the tithe is still 10 percent of your income. People often ask, "Is that 10 percent of the gross or net?" I always say, "We are foolish if we try to cheat God! Do we want a net blessing or a gross blessing from God?"

What is the meaning of "food in my house"? This is called the biblical way of sharing the wealth. One of the problems I have with the church today is that we pray for *God* to save starving children. Some people even say, "Well, if God is so all-powerful and loving, why does God allow children to starve?" God doesn't allow children to starve; *we* allow children to starve! You see, God's economy is that if all God's people bring a tenth of what they possess, then there will be food for everyone around the world. If every church in America would make the commitment to give money for food somewhere in the world where it is needed, just imagine the difference that would make. But here is the sad fact: Only 9 percent of all born-again adults tithe, according to a Barna Group survey conducted in 2007 ("New Study Shows Trends in Tithing and Donating," April 14, 2008). I'll say it again: The greatest fool of all is the person who believes that God exists but who lives as though God's directives don't matter.

God continues in Malachi 3:10, saying, "Test me in this . . . and see if I will not throw open the floodgates of heaven and pour out so much blessing that you will not have room enough for it" (NIV). God is saying to God's children, "*Test me.*" We must test God. The promise is that if we will tithe,

We must believe with our minds, trust with our hearts, and then release with our hands.

there will not be enough room to store all the blessings we will have.

In the next verse, God also promises that God will prevent pests from devouring our crops and the vines in our fields from dropping their fruit before it is ripe (Malachi 3:11). We do not need to be worried about our families during this downturn in the economy because God has promised to protect our crops! In other words, God will ensure we have some means of providing for our families. This promise is for anyone who trusts God enough to give as God has directed. We must believe with our minds, trust with our hearts, and then release with our hands.

2. Seek wise counsel through an accountability group or counselor.

So many temptations come against us in the area of finances. We need the accountability of a financial advisor or group. Groups such as Crown Financial Ministries and Dave

Ramsey's Financial Peace University have helped so many people. My wife, Carolyn, and I have a team of financial investors who meet with us twice a year and send us quarterly reviews. Recently, we received a report indicating how they had rebalanced some of our investments. They have made such a positive difference for us.

If professional accountability is not an option for you, many churches and community programs offer financial instruction, encouragement, and accountability through various classes and small groups. Another option is to consider starting an accountability or support group of your own, inviting a few trusted individuals or couples to meet with you weekly or biweekly for a designated period of time. There are numerous workbooks and study materials available for such groups. The important thing is to join together with one or more individuals who can offer insights, encouragement, and support for the journey. As Proverbs 15:22 says, "Plans fail for lack of counsel, / but with many advisors they succeed" (NIV). We can't do it by ourselves.

3. Write or rework a budget.

You can't spend what you don't have. With a budget, you are making a commitment to know where your money goes and thereby spend less than what you make. Everyone needs a budget. If you don't have one, you don't have to continue to "live" there! You can create a simple budget and begin to get your monthly spending on track.

One of the simplest ways to start a budget is to use the 10-10-80 formula. The first 10 percent of what you make goes to God, as we've already discussed. The next 10 percent goes into investing for your future. You pay yourself after you pay God. The remaining 80 percent is what you have left for living expenses.

Another helpful budgeting tool is the envelope method. One of the most liberating days in our financial life was about twenty-five years ago when Carolyn and I attended an all-day seminar on finances and were introduced to the envelope method. In this method you designate an envelope for every category in your budget, such as mortgage, utilities, groceries, entertainment, tithing/giving, gifts, spending money, and so forth. Then you put money or a check for the budgeted amount in each envelope. Once that money is gone, it's gone! Using plastic isn't an option. You can use only the money in the envelopes, and you can't borrow from one envelope to pad another.

Here's how it works. Let's say you've been to see a movie and want to get something to eat afterward, but you only have a couple of dollars left in the entertainment envelope. So you decide to go home and make spaghetti instead. (Carolyn and I actually did that once!)

Or let's say that you set aside so much money a month for vacation. The following summer you have saved $900, and so you tailor your travel plans to that amount of money. You spend only what you have, remembering that plastic is never an option.

Years ago when I was in graduate school, Carolyn and I took a three-night trip to Florida with another couple. We had to spend the first night in a tent because we didn't have enough money to get a hotel room for three nights. So, we drove all night to Disney World, set up the tent, spent all that day at Disney World, and then slept in the tent. The next morning we got in the car and drove to Daytona Beach. We were so beat by this time that we spent those two nights in a motel. Then we drove all the way back home. What a bargain it was for $89! (Remember, I said it was *years* ago!) We spent only what we had to spend, and we made it work.

The envelope system has worked very well for us through the years. Today we use a "virtual envelope" system by doing our budgeting and tracking of expenses using a computer software program. Although this electronic system works for us, some people find that it requires more discipline because you must keep track of your receipts and record every expenditure as it arises. (Online banking software also records your transactions, but it may not create any more discipline than a credit card statement.) Find what works for you. The important step is to have some sort of method or plan.

Even when Carolyn and I were using the physical envelopes, sometimes we had our problems. We would think we were doing well, and then we'd come up short. I would ask, "Carolyn, what happened?" And she would say that the insurance bill came due—you know, that bill you pay every six months.

We discovered that we needed to figure our insurance payment as a monthly category, setting aside a designated amount each month so that we would have the full amount when the bill was due. That's what I call "reworking the budget," making adjustments to fit our particular situation. And that helped us so much.

Reworking a budget is often necessary when there are income changes or adjustments, when there are cost of living increases due to inflation or fluctuations in the economy, when you add or omit activities or lessons such as piano or dance or soccer, and so forth. Oftentimes, reworking a budget will require you to make decreases in spending, which we will discuss at length in the next chapter.

Whether you are writing a budget for the first time or reworking an existing budget, be sure to allow a savings category for future needs. For example, we need new windows on our house. The old windows look terrible, but we're not going to buy new windows this year because we haven't saved all of the money for them. Plastic is not an option. As long as the windows don't leak, we're good; and if they start leaking a little, there's something called a caulking gun! The good news is that we won't be in debt. So, our current budget includes a category for new windows, and we set aside a little money each month. Our goal is to have enough money for new windows next year. If it takes longer for some reason, that's fine. We will just continue saving until we have enough. I will say more about saving for future needs later in the chapter.

4. Perform plastic surgery and reduce your debt.

Plastic surgery—cutting up your credit cards—is a commitment to an aggressive debt reduction program. To be faithful and obedient with what God has given you, you must deal with your debt. Debt is not God's will for your life. The Bible says we should never be the borrower but we should always be the lender. Proverbs 22:7 tells us why: "The rich rule over the poor, / and the borrower is the slave of the lender." Jesus died to set you free, but as long as you owe even a dollar to someone, you will always be a slave to that person.

Debt is not God's will for your life.

Carolyn and I have no debt other than our home mortgage. So when I checked our credit report, I couldn't understand why it wasn't perfect. I called to inquire about it, and I was told the reason for the less-than-perfect credit report is because we have twelve credit cards. I explained that we don't have a balance on any of them. But they said it doesn't matter. Every credit card has a credit limit, and so there's the possibility that we could go out tonight and charge up to that limit. Let's say, for example, that each card has a limit of $3,000. That is a total of $36,000 in potential credit, which is counted against us. When I asked what I could do to improve my credit rating, they suggested that we keep only one or two credit cards.

When you perform plastic surgery, the idea is to get rid of every card you don't need. Some individuals, for example, need a credit card for business or travel expenses. In that case, that credit card should be used for those purposes only, and the balance should be paid off each month. If you cannot exercise this kind of discipline, then you should cut up all of your cards! Remember, credit can become an addiction. If you have trouble eating too much candy, you don't want to keep the candy dish around. Likewise, if you have trouble overspending on credit, you don't need to keep a credit card around.

Some people argue that a credit card is necessary for "emergencies" only. The danger here is that it can be tempting to justify many things as "emergencies." Where do you draw the line? Besides, who wants to pay interest on an emergency? My recommendation is to set up an emergency fund for emergencies and cut up the plastic! (We will discuss setting up an emergency fund in Chapter 3.)

After you have cut up your credit cards, be sure that you call the credit card companies to cancel them. Be forewarned that they will try to talk you out of canceling. You know how it is when you go to a store and they say, "You can save 25 percent today if you will open a store credit card." You think to yourself, *What I'm buying costs $80, and 25 percent of $80 is a chunk.* Then they have you! Well, credit card companies will try similar tactics. So be firm in your decision. Cut up your cards and cancel them. Get rid of them!

Of course, you will need to pay off your remaining credit card balances, as well as begin to attack other debt. We will discuss in detail how to begin a debt reduction program in the next chapter.

5. *Set future goals and practice delayed gratification.*

Jeremiah 29:11 says, "For surely I know the plans I have for you, says the LORD, plans for your welfare and not for harm, to give you a future with hope." The Bible also says that "faith is the assurance of things hoped for, the conviction of things not seen" (Hebrews 11:1). When we use plastic, we're not practicing faith in God's Word. We're essentially saying, "I don't want to wait for a future blessing; I want it now." One of the most powerful disciplines of faith is the discipline of delayed gratification.

> **For surely I know the plans I have for you, says the LORD, plans for your welfare and not for harm, to give you a future with hope.**
> (Jeremiah 29:11)

We live in a world of instant everything. We are conditioned to think, "I want it right now." We are a generation of fast food and high-speed Internet and credit cards. But character is not instant. Character is developed through delayed gratification, which requires discipline. And delayed gratification begins in our finances. If we cannot practice delayed gratification in our finances, we cannot practice it in other areas of our lives.

At age forty-five I started a motorcycle account, and at age fifty-four I was able to put the cash down on that motorcycle. Although I had to wait nine years, the waiting made that motorcycle mean so much more than it would have meant if I had gone out and bought it on credit. It also means more because it is paid in full!

The couch in our living room is twenty-three years old. It's never used, so it looks pretty nice; it's just not what's in style today. I could live with this couch, but Carolyn wants to start a couch account—sort of like my motorcycle account. And because I want to be married for fifty years or more, I have agreed to this goal! Another goal of ours is redoing the kitchen. So we are saving for these two goals. We are practicing delayed gratification.

Delayed gratification plays an important role in financial planning.

Sometimes when we practice delayed gratification, we change our minds in the meantime. This keeps us from wasting our money on stuff we later would decide we didn't want or need. So whether we save for a future goal or change our minds and decide to use the money on something else, delayed gratification plays an important role in financial planning.

6. Nurture an attitude of gratitude.

The apostle Paul wrote, "I have learned to be content with whatever I have. I know what it is to have little, and I know what it is to have plenty" (Philippians 4:11-12). I'm always practicing this concept. It's easy for me to be negative sometimes. One time I missed my flight out of Chicago by ten minutes, so I had to spend the night in Chicago. My first thought was, *Oh, great!* But then I began to praise God for the possibilities in my experience of being stuck in Chicago for an evening.

When gas prices were so high recently, I was paying $4.07 per gallon to fill up my vehicle. Perhaps you had to pay more in your area. I happen to drive an SUV, so it cost me about $70 to fill up. When I would fill it up, watching the dollars add up so quickly, I would stand there and think, *This vehicle has 92,000 miles on it, but I'll probably have to drive it another five years.* Why? Because we pay cash for our vehicles, and we need new windows on our house! But do you know what I would say to myself every time I put another gallon of gas in the tank? *It's paid for.* You see, it's a whole lot cheaper driving something that gets twelve miles to the gallon than it would be buying something that gets fifty miles to the gallon but comes with a monthly payment. That's what I call nurturing an attitude of gratitude!

Be grateful for what you have and practice contentment. This one principle alone will do wonders for your finances.

7. Pray, pray, pray.

The most important right action you can take is prayer. Let's look again to the fourth chapter of James. He writes, "Draw near to God, and he will draw near to you" (verse 8). That's a promise. But what does it mean to draw near to God?

If my wife, Carolyn, and I were on opposite sides of the room, and I decided to walk over and stand beside her, my focus would be on one thing: Carolyn. I would be looking at her, and all my actions would be taking me nearer to her. Prayer is very similar. It is not just making a casual nod at God, as we often are accustomed to doing. It literally is directing all our energy toward God.

James continues, "Cleanse your hands, you sinners, and purify your hearts, you double-minded. Lament and mourn and weep. Let your laughter be turned into mourning and your joy into dejection" (4:8-9). Immediately after talking about drawing near to God, James talks about repentance. Drawing near to God through prayer involves repentance. We must ask ourselves, *Where do I need to redirect my priorities? What directives has God given me that I have not submitted to?* Then we must literally let our hearts ache for the things that cause God's heart to ache.

In the tenth verse, James writes, "Humble yourselves before the Lord, and he will exalt you." This is the act of putting ourselves in the place of total submission and total humility. When we humble ourselves before the Lord in prayer, he exalts us—he lifts us up.

Instead of relying upon our own abilities and ideas and energy, prayer appeals to our powerful parent who has promised to provide. Prayer acknowledges that we are dependent upon God and that we trust God to lead, guide, and provide. As we live in the place of total humility, submission and dependence on God, it just makes sense that the right results—God's results—will be brought about in our lives.

Seven Right Actions

1. Do the first "right" thing: planned giving to God.

2. Seek wise counsel through an accountability group or counselor.

3. Write or rework a budget.

4. Perform plastic surgery and reduce your debt.

5. Set future goals and practice delayed gratification.

6. Nurture an attitude of gratitude.

7. Pray, pray, pray.

Right Results

Right priorities + right actions = right results. It's a proven formula. When we combine right priorities with right actions, we are guaranteed to produce right results. First, we set right priorities based on God's directives; next, we implement those priorities by taking right actions; and then we begin to see positive results. The formula holds true in every area of our lives; and in the area of finances, the results impact every dimension of our lives. "Right results" not only means freedom from debt and financial health; it also means improved family dynamics, stronger relationships, and spiritual growth.

Remember, faith without works is dead. It's useless, powerless. So, I invite you to accept a two-step challenge. First, identify where you need to adjust your priorities. Are you trying to live with a foot in two conflicting worldviews? Second, identify where you need to make corrective action. Which of the seven right actions are you not currently practicing?

I acknowledge that this is no simple challenge. It's going to be hard. But it will bring right results! If you will prayerfully review your priorities and commit to these seven right actions for six months, you will begin to experience the power of God through financial freedom. Ask God to give you the strength you need to keep working at it until you reach your desired goals.

DU IT TODAY

Do It Today

Come now, you who say, "Today or tomorrow we will go to such and such a town and spend a year there, doing business and making money." Yet you do not even know what tomorrow will bring. What is your life? For you are a mist that appears for a little while and then vanishes. Instead you ought to say, "If the Lord wishes, we will live and do this or that." As it is, you boast in your arrogance; all such boasting is evil. Anyone, then, who knows the right thing to do and fails to do it, commits sin. (James 4:13-17)

Today we are reaping the harvest of the seeds we sowed yesterday. Think about that for a moment. What does that mean for you personally?

For me, it means that I am experiencing the harvest of a commitment I made in 1969 to get straight spiritually and be a radical disciple of Jesus Christ. And that's how I understood it when I made my commitment to Christ—that it is radical. Radical means "back to the roots." I decided I wasn't going to be just a "church person." I decided that whatever Jesus demands of my life and however many times I fail, I will never quit. So, today I'm living in the harvest of the seeds I sowed yesterday.

If you are married, you chose your spouse. You made a decision in the past, and today you are reaping the blessings or the curses that have come from that choice. You are experiencing today the harvest of the seeds you sowed yesterday.

Carolyn and I made a decision over thirty years ago that we would give to God the first 10 percent of everything that came into our hands, and today we're reaping the harvest of the seeds we sowed yesterday.

The area of finances happens to be one area of my life that I've done pretty well in throughout my adult years. But that may not be the case for you. You may be experiencing debt and other financial problems right now because of seeds you sowed in the past. Although you can't change the past, there's good news: The commitments and actions you make today will become the seeds that will create your harvest tomorrow. We can influence our tomorrow harvests! So it is critical that we make strategic plans for the future. That's the key to successful living. The way to begin experiencing success is to strategically plan for a purposeful future, and this is certainly true in the area of your personal finances. Let's explore what this involves.

One of the most important things about planning for tomorrow is realizing that we are not in control.

Plan According to God's Will

One of the most important things about planning for tomorrow is realizing that we are not in control. Life is so fragile, and it can turn in a moment. Accidents, terminal illness, unemployment—the list of unpredictable, life-altering experiences could go on and on.

James says that our lives are like a mist that vanishes (4:14). I was thinking about that description one morning as I was drinking a cup of coffee and looking out our back window. We have a little fishpond in our backyard, and on cool mornings steam comes off the pond. I thought to myself, *Gosh, that's how short life is.* That's why we're not to boast about tomorrow, for we don't know what a day may bring.

I came to a new understanding of this truth a number of years ago when I was flying home after speaking at a conference in Sacramento. I had flown from Sacramento to Chicago and had caught a connecting flight from Chicago to Dayton. We took off and were at cruising altitude when all of a sudden the plane made a sharp jerk. Both the beverage cart and the flight attendants fell over. When the plane righted, I heard a pop like the sound of an air gun, and the oxygen masks dropped. I knew that wasn't a good sign. Then we went into a forty-second dive. Recall the steepest drop you've ever experienced on a roller coaster, and then imagine sustaining that drop for forty seconds.

Fortunately, I was able to think clearly and put on the oxygen mask. Then I began to think all kinds of things. One thing I remember thinking was, *This is it. Am I going to feel the impact? Is this going to hurt?* Finally, at 8,000 feet, the pilot pulled out. He said that he didn't know what had happened, and he told us that we could take off the masks because we could breathe without assistance at 8,000 feet. Then he said he was going to try to make it back to Chicago, which was about thirty minutes away. He told us that if that wasn't possible, he would announce where he was going to try to set the plane down. That was the weirdest half hour in my life! One thing I learned for certain is that life is fragile, and we never know when it's going to end.

Because life is fragile and uncertain, planning for tomorrow is critical. Though it may seem that James is against planning for tomorrow, he's not. What James is saying is that we need to plan for tomorrow *according to God's will*. He writes, "Instead you ought to say, 'If the Lord wishes, we will live and do this or that' " (4:15). In other words, we must continually seek God's will and adjust our plans accordingly.

Planning for financial health in accordance with God's will is extremely important, because so often we allow our finances to be driven by pleasure addictions. Pleasure addictions are things we seek apart from God in an attempt to meet our needs or solve our problems, such as alcohol, drugs, unhealthy sex, and spending. That's right: Spending is just as much of an addiction as alcohol, drugs, or unhealthy sex.

In Luke 12:16-21, Jesus tells the story of a foolish investor who is blessed with abundance financially. Let's pause a moment and let that soak in. God *wants* to bless people financially, but it's always for God's purpose, God's will.

This guy is blessed, but he doesn't realize that it is God who gives us the ability to make wealth. He doesn't understand the source of his blessing. So he decides to build bigger barns so that he can accumulate more. He is working for the wrong reason; he is working toward building a secure retirement. What he fails to do is to involve God in the planning. And the results are disastrous.

We must always ask ourselves: Does my financial strategy align with God's will? In other words, does my financial strategy align with God's desires and directives for my life as expressed in God's Word? That's the important question.

Activate the Fundamental Life Principles of Sowing and Reaping

A lot of people have plans but fail to act on them. Once we have a plan, we must take action. In every area of life, and especially in the area of finances, we must activate the fundamental life principals of sowing and reaping.

In the apostle Paul's letter to the Galatians, we read: "Do not be deceived; God is not mocked, for you reap whatever you sow. If you sow to your own flesh, you will reap corruption from the flesh; but if you sow to the Spirit, you will reap eternal life from the Spirit" (6:7-8). When we sow to satisfy our pleasures, we experience chaos and destruction. Anytime we feed our passions or desires, we are going to reap destruction. But when we sow to please the Spirit, we reap eternal life. That word *eternal* doesn't simply mean life in heaven. It means not only *quantity* of life but also *quality* of life. If I were to live the way I used to live when I had an addiction, the quality of my life would be hell. But now that I am sowing to the Spirit, I am reaping the harvest of a good quality of life.

We will reap a harvest if we don't give up. It's a guarantee.

The next two verses in the Galatians passage give us even more motivation for sowing to the Spirit: "So let us not grow weary in doing what is right, for we will reap at harvest time, if we do not give up. So then, whenever we have an opportunity, let us work for the good of all, and especially for those of the family of faith" (6:9-10). Did you catch it? We *will* reap a harvest if we don't give up. It's a guarantee.

Let's consider, then, the specific life principles of sowing and reaping that we should activate in our lives.

1. You reap what you sow.

When you put seed in the ground, the fruit of that seed will be of like kind. If you put an apple seed into the ground, you are going to get an apple tree. If you put dandelion seeds into the ground, you are going to get dandelions. You always reap what you sow. So, if your attitudes and actions are the "seeds" that are going to create your future harvest, you better be sure that you are planting right attitudes and good actions.

As you think about your financial future, one of the greatest gifts you have is your ability to work. A job is a good thing. But every time you say something negative about your work, you are sowing negative seed. Remember, seed produces like kind. So negative comments will reap a negative result. Many companies today are cutting back and downsizing, and what do you think they are looking at as they evaluate their employees? They are looking to see which employees are planting good seeds and which are planting bad seeds.

What are some of the good seeds we want to make sure we're putting in the ground every day? The first one is *integrity*. Honesty is so important in every area of life, and certainly in our finances. Another is *attentiveness to detail*. Paying attention to details can make a big difference when it comes to working toward financial health. *Initiative* is another good seed. Who is the first one to work and the last one to leave? Who works through the lunch hour? Employers pay attention to those who demonstrate initiative. Then there's *excellent service*, *timeliness*, and *risk taking*. Risk-taking, in particular, is a seed we must be intentional to plant.

Given the current economic environment, it's easy to be cautious. We don't want to take risks. But when we're *too* cautious, it's as if we are leaving our seed on the shelf. Do you know what the Bible says happens to seed that's left on the shelf? It dries up and dies. While everyone else is being overly cautious, it is very important that we continue to put good seeds into the ground and make wise investments for retirement. If we don't continue putting seed in the ground now, then we won't have a sufficient harvest once the economy turns around. We need our seeds to be working for us now so that we will have a bountiful future harvest.

This is an important time to be putting good seeds into the ground.

2. *You determine the size of the harvest at the time of planting.*

A second life principle of sowing and reaping is that you determine how much you will harvest at the time of planting. The Bible puts it this way: "The one who sows sparingly will also reap sparingly, and the one who sows bountifully will also reap bountifully" (2 Corinthians 9:6). Do you want to sow sparingly, or are you going to sow generously?

When financial advisors do budget counseling, they talk about the 10-10-80 formula. I introduced this formula briefly in Chapter 2. The first 10 percent represents your giving. Carolyn and I made the commitment many years ago to give God the first 10 percent of everything that comes into our hands, and today we are reaping the harvest of the seed we sowed yesterday. Perhaps you have not sowed that seed, but you can begin to sow that seed today so that you will reap a harvest tomorrow. God promises that as you give, so it will be given back to you. Jesus said, "Give, and it will be given to you. A good measure, pressed down, shaken together, running over, will be put into your lap; for the measure you give will be the measure you get back" (Luke 6:38).

> **Give, and it will be given to you. . . . for the measure you give will be the measure you get back.**
> (Luke 6:38)

The next 10 percent of your income goes into investing for a promising future. Some people talk about retirement, but I like to talk about the life transition when we move to the next plan that God has for us. You see, we were not created to ever "quit." We just move to the next step in our God call. So, you must invest the second 10 percent of your income for the future.

Many companies have a matching program for 401(k) contributions. For example, if you contribute 3 percent to your 401(k), they will match up to 3 percent. That's 6 percent of your income you can invest tax free! Yet so many employees don't take advantage of this benefit. They're leaving money on the table. Remember, you determine the size of the harvest at the time of planting.

The third number in the formula represents 80 percent of your income, which is the money you have left for living expenses. As you grow in discipline, the first two categories should increase: your ability to give more than 10 percent to the Lord and to save more than 10 percent. What kind of promising future do you want to have? That's how much seed you are to put out there. Also, the idea is not to live off the whole 80 percent, because you want to have the opportunity to bless others as needs arise.

The 10-10-80 principle is a helpful guideline when planning how much of your income to give, save, and spend. When times are tough, it can be tempting to decrease the amounts you give and save so that you can increase the amount you have for expenses, but this demonstrates a lack of trust in God's provision. Instead, we should make sacrifices in the area of expenses while continuing to save and give, trusting God to meet all our needs. It is important to remember that nothing good comes without sacrifice. Even our salvation came at the great sacrifice of God's Son. We can't expect to coast our way to success. This is why it's so important to set future goals.

I like to write out my goals, including my financial goals, stating where I want to be in three years, five years, ten years, and twenty years. Ten years ago, I wrote goals for the next twenty years of my life. I listed them under the categories of missional goals and personal goals. Under missional goals, I wrote local church pastor followed by publishing, speaking, and seminars, which are both local and global in nature. I'm half-way through this twenty-year-plan, and I've written four books and conducted numerous seminars and speaking engagements. One of my personal goals was to have my children's education paid for by 2007. Because my son did not go to graduate school right after college but taught for three years first, I have had to extend that date a little bit. My other goal was to have a mountain home by 2004, and we built it in 2007. The Bible says that as we think, so we become (Proverbs 23:7, KJV). A similar truth is that the amount we sow determines the amount we reap.

As you begin to set your own goals and plant seeds for the future, remember that you are determining the size of your harvest at the time of planting, which goes hand in hand with the next principle.

3. You will reap more than you sow.

Not only will you determine the size of the harvest at the time of planting; you also will reap *more* than you sow. You see, there is a principle of creation at work in sowing and reaping. In telling the parable of the sower, Jesus said, "Other seeds fell on good soil and brought forth grain, some a hundredfold, some sixty, some thirty" (Matthew 13:8).

Rather than simply feeding the hungry, many churches and mission groups seek to create a sustainable agricultural program. They know that if you just feed people, you create consumers. But if you empower farmers, you are empowering creators. I don't want to win the lottery. If I win the lottery, I'm a consumer. That doesn't do me or my future generations any good, nor does it bless anyone around me. No, I want to be empowered to be a creator, because we reap more than we sow.

The same principle works in reverse in regards to debt. Let's say you owe $5,560 on your credit card. That's about equivalent to one trip for a family of four to Disney World, plus a three-day cruise. The interest on a typical credit card is 18 percent. Read the fine print on your credit card agreements. The average late fee is $29, plus your interest rate increases. With many credit cards, your rate goes to 23.4 percent when you are late in making a payment. Your credit card company has a guaranteed rate of return: 18 percent of what you continue to owe. So you pay $1,000 a year in interest on the amount that has a minimum payment of $80 a month. Most people pay only the minimum payment; so at the end of forty years you still owe the initial amount. You took a trip to Disney World forty years ago, and you still haven't paid for it. You have merely paid $1,000 a year interest to the shareholders in the credit card company. Your credit card company during that forty years charged compounded interest at 18 percent and made over $40,000 from your $5,560 investment. Talk about reaping more than you sow!

Let's say that you took that same $80 a month you pay to the credit card company and invest it at 12 percent (which over the long term of forty years is an honest return). Because of the miracle of compound interest, in forty years you would make roughly $952,193 (tax deferred). Instead of giving that money to credit card companies, you could invest it and become a future millionaire!

Compound interest is our friend! For our son's college, Carolyn and I put something into mutual funds every month from the time he was born until he was in fifth grade. Because of commitments to God's mission, from fifth grade on we did not save for college anymore. We had put in $5, $10, and $25 as we went along, and by the time he was in fifth grade, we had put $1,000 in his college fund. With mutual funds that became $4,000 by the time he graduated high school.

You may be saying, "Wait a minute. I have lost 40 percent of my investment since the stock market decline." Many are in the same situation. Market loss, however, is not the same as market fluctuation. If you didn't cash in, you haven't lost anything. Since the 1800s, the market has always come back. It has gone down thirty-one times on an average of every five years. As long as you don't touch it, you have only experienced market fluctuation, not market loss. Just be sure that you are diversified, which will allow you to get multiple returns, and hang in there for the long term. Also, it is always a good idea to seek out the advice of a wise investment consultant.

4. The harvest comes in a later season than the sowing.

A farmer plants seeds in early spring and harvests crops in the fall. There is a period of waiting between planting and harvesting. The same is true in the area of finances. It takes time to save and to invest and to watch money grow. The problem is that we don't want to wait. We want it now. And that leads to debt. When we do it God's way, the harvest comes in a later season than the sowing.

If we want to experience the maximum harvest, we must have patience and perseverance. Remember, Galatians 6:9 encourages us to not to become weary in doing good, because we will reap a harvest at just the right time if we do not give up. I love the way the writer of Hebrews describes perseverance: "Let us run with endurance the race that is set before us, fixing our eyes on Jesus, the author and perfecter of faith" (12:1-2, NASB). This is the only way to realize financial health—day by day, moment by moment, as we keep our eyes fixed on Jesus Christ.

5. *You are responsible for the work of sowing; God is responsible for the harvest.*

As we are faithful to do the hard work of sowing, God will be faithful for the harvest. Much of the "hard work" of sowing comes in creating a sound strategy for your financial future based on biblical principles. In other words, it is creating a financial plan. When you make a commitment to create a financial plan and follow it through, God will bring the harvest.

This principle is illustrated so well in the story of a young couple, Lance and Amber. Lance shares the story with us in his own words:

> *Amber and I met in college and got married and right away we started to live off credit cards. Debt just started to build. We didn't have any sense of a budget. We had no idea of where our money was going. And so by the time we graduated from college, the debt was getting bigger and bigger. The more we would try to say, "Well, we're just going to spend less," nothing would happen because we didn't have a plan.*
>
> *After three years of law school we moved here. Just our credit card debt, not including our student loans, was at $20,000. The only thing we really had to show for it was a washer and dryer and our bed. Everything else was spent on eating or going to the movies or buying gifts for other people at Christmas. We were working to pay off stuff we didn't even have anymore.*
>
> *Once we got to our church, we heard a series of messages about stewardship and signed up for a commitment campaign. But then we faced a dilemma, which was: How much do we give versus how much do we use to get out of debt? We prayed*

about it, and talked about it, and finally came to the conclusion that we're going to give as if we don't have the debt and we will work our debt reduction around our giving. So we started giving 10 percent. We thought that was what we should do.

We sat down and had a serious "budget" meeting. For each month we set "X amount of dollars" aside for this and "X amount of dollars" aside for that. For eating out, it was $30 a month. We'd go out to eat once. For personal spending money, it was ten bucks a month. If you wanted something that was $50, you were going to have to wait five months. It was brutally hard. That's just how it had to be.

The numbers don't add up. There's no other explanation for us, other than it was God taking care of us because we were now walking in the road that God wanted us to walk. We had the resources to give. We had the resources to get out of debt, and we didn't go without what we needed.

Neither one of us got any raises. Amber works as a teacher and I work for the county. As lawyers go, I don't make a third of what I could make at a private firm if I had gone that route. But somehow those loaves and fishes multiplied to where the debt is dead and we gave more than we thought we ever could have given.

Amber's car is now paid for. It's phenomenal. It's an extra bunch of money each month that we didn't have yesterday. Amber and I have been married about nine and a half years; we're now expecting our first child in a couple months. When that baby comes, we're not going to still be sending most of our money each month to pay for movies we went to see in college. We can use that money to provide for our child. And instead of looking backward all the time each month, our finances and our lives can be looking forward to whatever God has in store for us.

As Lance and Amber discovered, God blesses our efforts when we do the work. And we cannot begin the work until we have a plan. Procrastination is the great robber of life. Don't put it off! Don't be a slave to debt any more. Make a commitment to create a financial plan and follow it through, and God will bring the harvest.

The Fundamental Life Principles of Sowing and Reaping

1. You reap what you sow.

2. You determine the size of the harvest at the time of planting.

3. You will reap more than you sow.

4. The harvest comes in a later season than the sowing.

5. You are responsible for the work of sowing; God is responsible for the harvest.

Now, let's walk through the steps in creating a financial plan together.

Create Your Financial Plan

1. Do a financial analysis.

The first step in creating a financial plan is to sit down and do a financial analysis. This helps you to see exactly where you are. The Bible says we must be sure to know the condition of our herds and crops—and I would add, our stocks!

First, list on paper all of your debt. Most people are unaware of the total sum of their debt. Debt includes house, car, bills, credit cards, student loans, and other loans. Most people underestimate what they owe by about two-thirds. For example, if you think you have $9,000 in consumer debt, you may actually owe $27,000. So be sure to add up everything. But don't pass out when you look at the figure because we have a big God! God is bigger than our debt or stupidity. I've experienced that in my own life! God's grace continues to be bigger than any of my mistakes or failures.

Next, list on paper all of your assets. Assets include things such as bank accounts, investments, possessions, and insurance. This will give you the total value of your money and property—your revenue and resources.

Now subtract the debts from the assets to determine your net worth. This will give you a picture of where you are financially and help you to pinpoint areas where adjustments need to be made. For example, it might help to identify where you should start attacking your debt, as well as which assets can be sold or "cashed in" to provide money for debt reduction—which leads to the next step in your financial plan.

2. Begin an aggressive program of debt reduction.

An aggressive and effective debt reduction program requires an intentional plan. If you have a significant amount of credit card debt, you will need a long-term plan to get out of debt, realizing that the first year you'll be able to pay down a portion, the next year you'll be able to pay down an additional portion, and so forth until you pay off the full amount. You might have a three-year plan, a five-year plan, a seven-year plan, or a ten-year plan, but creating and maintaining that plan promises light at the end of the tunnel. Send your creditors a copy of your plan, and most creditors will back off. They want their money, and you've got a plan. They don't really want you to declare bankruptcy, and your plan shows good faith. Christians should show good faith and do everything possible to avoid declaring bankruptcy.

Paying off smaller debts yields a greater sense of accomplishment, so start with the smaller debts. Then build on that momentum by putting your monthly debt reduction amount toward the next smallest debt, adding in any extra money you can.

One of the best ways to find additional money for paying off debt is to reduce your expenses. Someone told me that his family spends $150 per month on cable TV. That $150 could go a long way in helping to reduce debt! You can live without cable TV for six months. Just get a converter box, and you will still be able to get five or six stations in Hi-Definition. Not only will your finances improve, relationships will improve as well as you spend less time watching TV. Another possibility is to get rid of your landline telephone. I know very few people under the age of thirty who have a landline telephone. Consider getting rid of newspapers and magazines for six months, and watch how that can help to eliminate debt in your life. Here's another one: Sell something that you are not using. Perhaps you have a boat—or a lawnmower or something else—that you rarely use. Sell some things you're not using and put that money toward debt reduction.

Another way to get additional money for paying off debt is to earn additional income. Too many people decide to get a second job earning minimum wage, but that may not bring the most effective results. Consider the skills you have that may be in some way marketable. Any number of possibilities can be nurtured within your talents. I've met people who, because they are computer-savvy, are building websites for organizations or small businesses. I know moms who have a daycare in their own homes. They are trained to watch two or three additional children and effectively add additional income without needing to pay for childcare themselves. Think of ways you can create additional income, and put that money toward debt reduction.

3. Create an emergency fund.

I remember when we had several emergencies in our household in a short period of time. First, our air conditioner went out. It had a ten-year guarantee on it, but we had owned the house more than ten years; so it cost us $3,000 to repair. Then we had to repair the outside of our house to fix where moisture got under the siding—another $3,000. Then my car broke down, and that was $500 to fix. In no time our monthly expenses jumped by $7,000. If we had not had an emergency fund, what would we have done? We would have pulled out the plastic.

If you have an emergency fund, you are prepared for those emergencies that inevitably come up; and you won't get caught in the cycle of debt. Most financial advisors recommend you start by saving $1,000 in an emergency fund. From there, you can continue saving until you have set aside three month's worth of income.

4. Be sure you have adequate life insurance.

The next thing to consider is life insurance. If you are a parent and still have children at home, you need to be sure you have adequate insurance to cover your children's well-being in the event that something should happen to you.

Remember the story of my flight from Chicago to Dayton? Believe it or not, another thought that went through my mind when the plane was dropping was, *We don't have adequate life insurance so that our children's education will be provided for!* The very next week we took out a term life insurance policy on me that would replace my income and provide for the needs of my family in the event of my death. (Term life insurance is less expensive than whole life insurance, and many people can get adequate coverage for several hundred dollars a year.)

We also took out a smaller term life insurance policy on Carolyn, because we have always used Carolyn's income to pay for our children's education. We determined the amount that would be needed to complete their education based on her income. Several years later, after they had completed their educations, we eliminated the amount that we were paying each month for Carolyn's policy because we no longer needed it.

Your life insurance needs, like ours, will change as your family's financial goals, needs, and resources change. The rule of thumb is to have enough life insurance to replace the financial value that each wage earner provides to the family. So, I don't worry about whether there will be enough money to bury me. They can bury me anywhere! The important thing is to ensure there is money to adequately care for the children.

5. Write a will.

If you are like most people, you either do not have a will, or the will that you have is invalid. Perhaps the witnesses are now deceased or the laws of your state have changed, making the document invalid. If you were to die today, the state would divide your assets among your surviving heirs as they see fit, after extracting probate costs, state inheritance taxes, and federal inheritance taxes. That's poor stewardship!

Would you rather spend a few hundred dollars in attorney costs, or have several times that amount in court costs to be deducted from your estate before your assets are distributed? A simple will can avoid these problems. (For larger estates, a trust may be more advantageous.)

For parents, a will is particularly important in designating legal guardians for your children. When our children were very young, Carolyn and I were going to fly to California for a conference. We were going to leave the children at home with friends. So we decided to sit down with our attorney and draw up a will. We wanted them to have the same spiritual foundation that we would provide, the same emphasis on education, and the same guidelines for dating only people of faith. So we carefully selected a couple in our church and asked them if they would be willing to take our children if something happened to us. This not only gave us great peace of mind, but it also provided for the future protection and security of our children.

To begin the process of creating or updating your will, visit some financial websites on the Internet (e.g., www.crown.org and www.daveramsey.com). Look for articles on the most commonly asked questions regarding wills and trusts. Then get in touch with an attorney and discuss options and fees. Although software programs are available to help you create your own will, it is recommended that you always have an attorney who thoroughly understands the laws of your state to proofread the final document to ensure that it is probatable in court.

6. Look at your giving.

Jesus said, "Where your treasure is, there your heart will be also" (Matthew 6:21). So it is important to prayerfully identify the gap between what you are currently giving and what you believe God wants to give through you. Then you must determine how you can close that gap. When we give first to God a portion of everything that comes into our hands, we are demonstrating that our trust is not in our own means. Our trust is not in our success. Our trust is in the Lord.

Some Christians ask me if giving to organizations such as the United Way or the police boosters is counted in biblical giving. I respond by explaining that biblical giving requires two components. First, it must honor God by making God more visible. Others see it and think or say what Jesus observed: "By this everyone will know that you are my disciples, if you have love for one another" (John 13:35). Biblical giving won't honor you; it will honor God. Second, it will be a blessing to other people.

7. Create a budget.

A budget is an essential component of every financial plan. In the previous chapter, I talked about writing or reworking a budget in which you designate how much you will spend each month in specific categories. A typical budget might include categories such as mortgage/rent, utilities, groceries, transportation/gas, insurance, entertainment, spending money, gifts, medical expenses, and so forth. As I've mentioned, the envelope system is an effective tool for managing a budget because it helps to keep you from spending more money than you have designated for a specific category—which enables you to live within your means. You actually put either cash or a check into each envelope, and that's all you have to spend for that category. If you are a little more disciplined, a computer program can be used in a similar way. But you have to keep up with your spending in each category and hold yourself accountable!

Carolyn and I have been doing this for years. If Christmas is coming up and we have $300 in the Christmas envelope (or in the Christmas category in the computer program), we know that's all we can spend. We are not people who will spend $1,000 to $2,500 at Christmas because we simply won't put it on plastic. That's our rule.

If we want to go on vacation, we try to put aside a hundred dollars or more a month, depending on the state of the economy. When I was paying $70 per tank to fill up my SUV, vacation savings had to decrease some. So, let's say that we are setting aside what we can for vacation, and when the time comes we have only $400 in the account or envelope designated for vacation. We're obviously not going to Florida! So we might do two nights in Gatlinburg, Tennessee, instead.

Again, the 10-10-80 principle is helpful when planning your budget. The first 10 percent is designated for giving to God—or, if you have gone beyond the tithe, it might be 15 percent for you, which means that you will need to adjust the percentage for living expenses. The next 10 percent is for savings and investments. For those of us in our fifties and sixties who have lost some of our retirement investments, the savings amount probably should be more like 20 or 25 percent! And again, this means we must adjust the percentage we have left to live on. The idea is to continually push ourselves in the areas of savings and, in particular, giving.

God calls us to exceed the limits of our comfort zone and to grow in our giving. This requires careful budgeting and living by the Spirit, which is doing the right thing rather than the self-satisfying or easy thing. A mountain climber puts metal stakes in the rock as he or she climbs. Even if the climber slips, he or she can never fall back farther than the last stake. So, every year set a "stake" and build layer upon layer so that you won't fall below your last commitment. Your budget may be the most critical tool of all as you make the climb toward financial health!

Steps in Creating a Financial Plan

1. Do a financial analysis.

2. Begin an aggressive program of debt reduction.

3. Create an emergency fund.

4. Be sure you have adequate life insurance.

5. Write a will.

6. Look at your giving.

7. Create a budget.

INVESTING IN GOD'S FUTURE HARVEST

4

INVESTING IN GOD'S FUTURE HARVEST

My brothers and sisters, whenever you face trials of any kind, consider it nothing but joy, because you know that the testing of your faith produces endurance. (James 1:2-3)

When I think of a harvest, I always think of Thanksgiving, the holiday whose origin dates back to 1621. The first Thanksgiving was essentially a proactive response of faith, a religious celebration. The Pilgrims had lost over half their population in a year's time, and they were facing a winter of extreme famine. They were sure to lose many more of their number, and yet they chose as an act of faith to give thanks.

As the people of God living in hard and uncertain times today, we too must choose to give thanks as an act of faith. When we do, we are investing in God's future harvest—in our own lives as well as the lives of others. In this final chapter we will consider three important ways we can invest all God has given us in God's future harvest.

Live and Give Thankfully

First, we must live and give *thankfully*, even in the midst of difficult circumstances. To unpack what this means, let's begin by looking again to the Book of James. In the first verse of the book, James identifies to whom he was writing: the Jewish Christians who were scattered throughout the world because they were being persecuted for their faith. As refugees, they were dealing with two incredible hardships. First, they had the economic hardship of leaving behind their work and possessions. All they took with them was whatever they could carry on their backs. That gave them a sense of homelessness. Their second hardship was persecution.

> **Trials are actually opportunities because they test our faith, which produces perseverance.**

In light of these two hardships, James writes, "My brothers and sisters, whenever you face trials of any kind, consider it nothing but joy, because you know that the testing of your faith produces endurance" (1:2-3). Isn't that amazing? Trials are actually opportunities because they test our faith, which produces perseverance.

As I mentioned in the introduction to this book, I have been investing in my 401(k) since 1972, and I have "lost" a sizeable chunk of this money in the recent economic downturn. But what gives me perspective is to consider how two-thirds of the rest of world lives. So, each year I go on a mission trip to connect with a corner of the other two-thirds of the world, and I always come to the same realization: I am blessed. You are blessed. If we have a roof over our heads and food to eat, we are blessed.

Not long ago I went with a mission team from our church to Jamaica. Average unemployment in America is 6.5 percent. Average unemployment in Jamaica is over 70 percent. In other words, fewer than 30 percent of the people in Jamaica have a job. One of the things we did while we were there was to check on those businesses and individuals our church has given loans to, as well as to interview entrepreneurs who have applied for a loan.

One afternoon I met Gary, a thirty-five-year-old fisherman. We have loaned Gary $400 to repair his boat and get the motor in working order. Currently, his only method of fishing is to use fishing poles. Gary has paid back his $400 loan ahead of time, and now he has requested $500 so that he can buy ten fishing traps. That way he not only will be fishing with poles but also with ten traps, which will increase his harvest.

Gary's mother died when he was seven, and he does not know his father. He has no living relatives other than his wife and baby. At the age of nineteen, he built a home out of scrap lumber that he found floating in the ocean. He would gather the lumber, clean it off, and dry it in the sun. His baby has asthma, and they have no medicine. So we took Gary and the baby to a clinic nearby where we got the baby an inhaler, and by that afternoon the baby was breathing normally.

Getting in touch with those who are less fortunate than we are gives us perspective. Of course, we don't have to go to another country to gain perspective and be grateful for what we have. A careful look at the needs in your own community will accomplish the same outcome. Perspective is crucial if we are to live and give thankfully. The result is that we recognize God as the rightful owner of all we have been given, and we desire to release all we have into God's hands for God's purposes.

Live and Give Faithfully

In addition to living and giving thankfully, we must live and give *faithfully*. Recent months have been challenging for businesses and individuals across our nation, and I believe the story found in Jeremiah 32 can help us to see the necessity of faithfulness in difficult times.

The first two verses in the chapter indicate that it is 588 B.C. Jerusalem is surrounded by the armies of Babylon, which is modern-day Iraq. King Zedekiah has arrested a prophet by the name of Jeremiah and is holding him prisoner in his courtyard. The king has arrested Jeremiah because he is a prophet of irritation. In other words, Jeremiah is prophesying against his own people, telling them that they are the problem. He says that their real enemy is not Babylon, which has them under siege, but themselves. Why? They have turned their backs on the living God and are serving idols made with human hands.

At the risk of being misunderstood as Jeremiah was in his day, I would like to suggest that what is happening in our nation's economy today is more than an economic correction; I believe it also is a spiritual correction because we have turned our backs on the living God and are serving idols we have created with our own hands. Despite our many advances, the truth is that we are not much different than the people of Jeremiah's day.

As we read in Jeremiah 32:6-7, God tells Jeremiah, through the voice of his uncle, that they are about to be taken away into slavery by the Babylonians, and that everything they possess, including the land of Israel, will soon belong to Babylon. The first Jews to return to the land will not return for another fifty years. Jeremiah will never come back, and he has only two weeks before he is to leave. Then God tells Jeremiah to do something that sounds insane: He is to take the money that is in his hand and invest it in a piece of real estate. Faith, however, doesn't always make sense. This is why we must live and give faithfully, not according to what makes sense.

Well, Jeremiah tells God that this doesn't make sense. Why should he buy real estate when the title to the land will be worthless in two weeks? Sounds kind of like investing in the stock market at the point of its worst decline, doesn't it? But here's what God was doing: God was telling Jeremiah to take the money in his hand and invest it in the place where God would produce a future harvest. That's the paradox of faith. God tells us to take what's in

That's the paradox of faith. God tells us to take what's in our hand and use it as seed in the ground today for God's harvest tomorrow.

our hand and use it as seed in the ground today for God's harvest tomorrow. To the spiritually uninitiated, this makes no sense. It seems irrational.

Later, in verse 24 of the same chapter, Jeremiah reflects on what is happening. He writes, "See how the siege ramps are built up to take the city. Because of the sword, famine, and plague, the city will be handed over to the Babylonians who are attacking it. What you said has happened, as you now see" (NIV). In that day, the enemy would use stones and dirt to build huge ramps; they could push catapults up these ramps and thus destroy a city. Jeremiah is observing that the destruction God has foretold is indeed coming to pass.

In the verses that follow, we read these words: "And though the city will be handed over to the Babylonians, you, O Sovereign LORD, say to me, 'Buy the field with silver and have the transaction witnessed.' Then the word of the LORD came to Jeremiah: 'I am the LORD, the God of all mankind. Is anything too hard for me?' " (32:25-27, NIV).

Sometimes God's directives don't make sense to us, but we are called to live by faith and not by sight. Living by faith is trusting God and believing nothing is impossible for God.

When we live and give in this way, we position ourselves to experience the blessings of God's future harvest.

Living faithfully is living free of fear and paralysis.

The opposite of living faithfully is living fearfully. Fear induces panic, and panic creates impulsive decision-making. Impulsive decision-making can lead to using credit and making bad investments. Bad decisions are born when we live out of fear, not out of faith. When we begin to live in fear and panic, we are tempted to lose integrity and do things we don't truly want to do, such as lie, steal, report false income to the government, or write bad checks. Even church people have been known to do such things; however, anytime we step outside the boundaries of God's integrity, God will not prosper us. God will never bless our poor choices.

Living faithfully is living free of fear and paralysis. Fear keeps us from making healthy decisions and keeps us in a perpetual cycle of debt and defeat, but I encourage you to believe God's Word and follow God's directives. God has given you or put within your reach all the resources you need. And if you're faithful and obedient with what God has given you, God will multiply it for God's purpose.

> **We are the living, breathing body of Christ. We are the only hands and feet that God has to do God's work in the world.**

Live and Give Sacrificially

Finally, we must live and give *sacrificially.* Many Christians have forgotten who we are. We are the living, breathing body of Christ. We are the only hands and feet that God has to do God's work in the world. You and I are God's economic delivery system. We are God's bank account.

I often hear pastors say, "God doesn't need your money. God can do it without your money." Actually, God does need your money. God not only needs your money; God needs your hands and feet, too. In fact, God needs *all* of you.

On one of our church mission trips, I was serving as the runner between the doctor, who determined what each individual's needs were, and the pharmacist. One prescription looked to me like a diabetic medicine, so I called out, "It says diabetes." The pharmacist's assistant started to get me medicine for diabetes, and then the pharmacist saw the paper and said, "No! Look at the blood test results here. You'd kill that person with that medication. He's a non-diabetic." God needed that pharmacist's hands in that place and at that time. She saved a person's life that day.

God needs your money. God needs your time. God needs your hands and feet. God needs all you have to give.

What I like about the Book of James is that he reminds us we are going to die. Stay with me here! He calls us a vanishing mist, and we need to be reminded of this (James 4:14). Jesus himself said our lives are like a seed. If all we do is hold on to that seed and use it for ourselves, it remains nothing more than a wasted seed that rots. But if we're willing to give it up and risk it to the ground of God's proposed harvest, it will yield a return for the kingdom of God that is thirty, sixty, or even one hundred times greater. This is why it is so important for every follower of Jesus Christ to live and give sacrificially. The salvation of others depends on every one of us choosing to live and give sacrificially—giving up not only our money but also our very lives to the ground of God's kingdom purpose so that others may know eternal life, which begins today and continues forever.

When we live and give sacrificially to God's kingdom work, we are helping to bring people to new life in Jesus Christ, and that should be the basis of what we're about as followers of Christ. Transformation in the lives of others should be the foundation of everything we do. That kind of "future harvest" is possible only through our sacrificial living and giving. Jesus asks us to give everything—our very lives. He said we must lose our lives in order to find them. He told us that if we want to follow him, we must deny ourselves and take up our cross daily. It's not a one-time decision, and it's not always easy. In fact, it's work! Yet despite the cost, a disciple continues to live and risk and act outside his or her comfort zone.

> **Transformation in the lives of others should be the foundation of everything we do. That kind of "future harvest" is possible only through our sacrificial living and giving.**

On one mission trip that Carolyn and I went on together, there were more dental patients than the one dentist on the team could see. So he said to Carolyn, "I really trust you. I'm going to need you to shoot some Novocain and maybe pull some teeth today, because we've got more people than I can personally see." Talk about moving outside your comfort zone! But Carolyn stepped up to the challenge and, under his direction, helped provide dental care to the people needing attention.

A disciple continually acts outside his or her comfort zone. Followers of Jesus Christ always attempt to do things with their lives that other people believe are impossible.

Four men are responsible for much of the mission work that our church is doing in Jamaica. I call them the fellowship of the ring. I call them that because they are one powerful discipleship group. Some incredible work has come out of their group. Not long ago they arranged for a woman in Jamaica to fly to Dayton, Ohio, for cataract surgery—at no cost to her. Can you believe that a discipleship group of four men who meet every other week got all of the resources together to do that? That's a true discipleship group—a group that serves and gives sacrificially out of their calling and giftedness.

We must dream God's dreams together.

When we are willing to live and give sacrificially, we can change the world one life at a time.

The problem is that so often we join friendship groups rather than discipleship groups. We get together to eat and socialize rather than to do anything for Jesus in the world. True disciples understand that you can't live a life of extraordinary faith and possibility by yourself; you've got to join together with others. We must dream God's dreams together and hold one another accountable. When we are willing to live and give sacrificially—both as individuals and as the body of Christ—we can change the world one life at a time.

I challenge you to step up to sacrificial living and giving. Close the gap between what you're currently giving of your resources, time, and energy and what you believe God wants to give through you. This is possible only by faith. If each of us will be obedient to God by faith, we can take the resources we have in our hands and release them to God's purposes so that we can transform the world one life at a time. May we give all that we are and all that we have into God's hands for God's purposes!

Rebalancing Your Life

How will you now re-evaluate your own priorities and rebalance your life both financially and spiritually? The author describes right actions (pp. 34–48) that, when combined with right priorities, lead to new and liberating results.

Right Actions

As you begin this next chapter in your own life, what changes will you make? What actions will you commit to? Write one sentence for each action below to describe changes you will make to change your world in the next twelve months.

1. Giving to God:

_____

_____

_____

_____

2. Learning:

_____

_____

_____

_____

3. Budgeting:

_____

_____

_____

_____

4. Reducing Debt:

_____

_____

_____

_____

5. Future Goals:

_____

_____

_____

_____

6. Being Grateful:

_____

_____

_____

_____

7. Prayer:

The most important right action you can take is to pray. God has offered the powerful support of a loving parent. Write a prayer that will bring you into God's presence each day as you ask for support and blessing on what you plan to do. Put the prayer in your Bible or on your mirror and pray these words each day.

_____

_____

_____

_____

_____

_____

_____

Commitment

How will you move toward freedom from debt that can inhibit your mission in the world? Make a commitment below to specific ways you can begin to save for the future and reduce existing debt.

• I will save for the future by:

_____

_____

_____

• I will reduce debt by:

_____

_____

_____

God's Future Harvest

The author says,

> Living by faith is trusting God and believing nothing is
> impossible for God. When we live and give in this way, we
> position ourselves to experience the blessings of God's
> future harvest. . . . We are the only hands and feet that God
> has to do God's work in the world. (pp. 86–87)

What is one specific way you can be God's hands and feet in
the world? Write your response below:

_____

_____

_____

_____

_____

_____

_____

_____

_____

_____

_____

_____

_____

_____

_____

_____